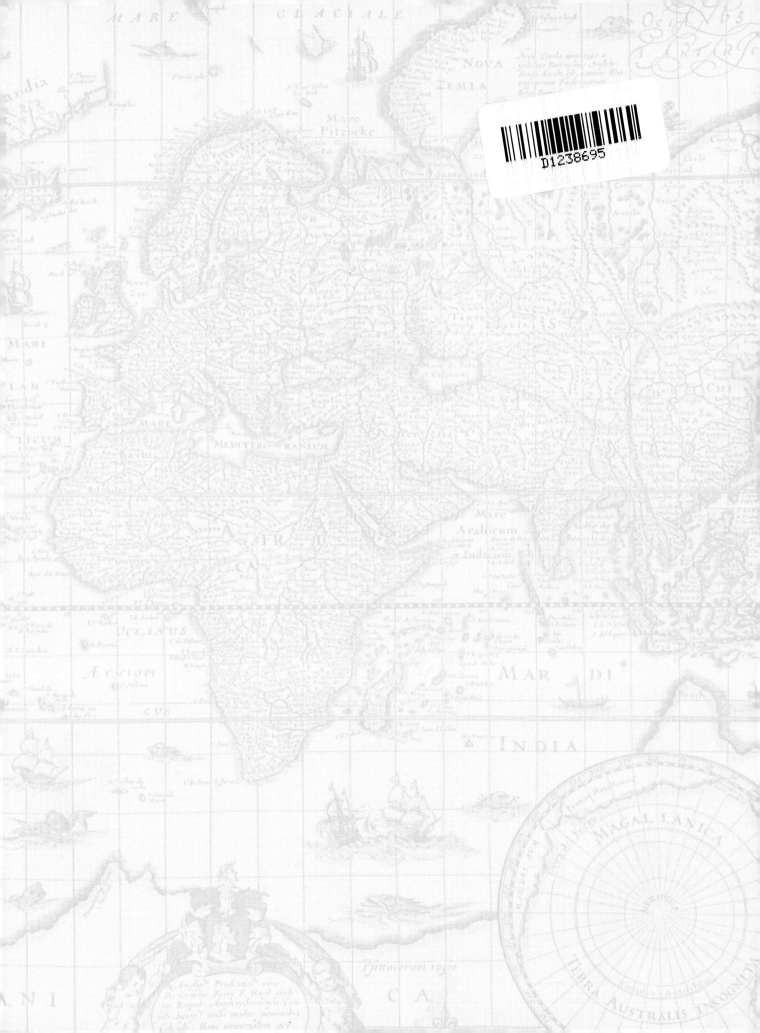

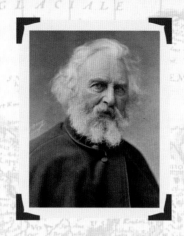

Nineteenth-century poet Henry Wadsworth Longfellow often took long walks beside the ocean. His favorite destination was the Portland Head Lighthouse, where he enjoyed lively conversations with its original keeper, Joshua Strout. Longfellow may have had the old stone tower and its keeper in mind when he wrote these words:

"Steadfast, serene, immovable,

The same year after year,

Through all the silent night,

Burns on forevermore,

That quenchless flame,

Shines on that inextinguishable light!

Sail on! It says, sail on,

Ye stately ships,

And with your floating bridge,

The ocean span:

Be yours to bring man nearer unto man."

Excerpt from: "The Lighthouse" by Henry Wadsworth Longfellow

Detail from "Map Light"

LIGHTHOUSES ON PARADE
Portland, Maine

A COMMUNITY ART PROJECT
PRESENTED BY HANNAFORD

PRINTED BY MONROE LITHO • ROCHESTER, NEW YORK
PAPER BY StoraEnso

For more information, visit the
Hannaford's Lighthouses on Parade Web site at
www.LighthousesOnParade.com.

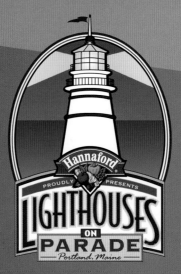

A COMMUNITY ART PROJECT
FOR THE GREATER PORTLAND AREA

A portion of the proceeds from the sale of this book will benefit
The American Lighthouse Foundation.

Design and Layout by Gretchen Bye, Dixon Schwabl Advertising
Written by Lou Ann Benigni-Lynch, Dixon Schwabl Advertising
Coordination by Jessica Savage and Jillian Eddinger, Dixon Schwabl Advertising
Production Supervision by Christina Williams, Dixon Schwabl Advertising
Photography by Dennis and Diana Griggs
Produced by Out Front Productions, LLC

Historical references courtesy of Tim Harrison,
President of The American Lighthouse Foundation

Monroe Litho, Official Printer for Hannaford's Lighthouses on Parade

ISBN 0-9711459-89

Table of Contents

LIGHTHOUSES—THE TRUE SYMBOL OF MAINE'S SPIRIT

For over two hundred years, lighthouses have been permanent guardians along the Maine coastline, shining their guiding light across the Atlantic. They have remained a steadfast symbol of the state's maritime lifestyle and rocky shores. Today, lighthouses are instantly recognizable icons that have come to represent pride and community spirit.

This symbolic meaning behind the lighthouse is one of the main reasons why Hannaford's Lighthouses on Parade is a natural fit for the Greater Portland region. And no one could agree more than Barbara Keefe from Maine Center on Deafness (MCD). During a visit to Rochester, New York in the summer of 2001, Barbara "fell in love" with the beautifully decorated horses that lined the streets. They were part of the Horses on Parade project, spearheaded by Lauren Dixon and Howie Jacobson. Soon afterward, she contacted the team—now known as Out Front Productions—and Hannaford's Lighthouses on Parade was born!

Like other community art projects featuring cows, moose, pigs and horses that have been so successful in world-class cities including Zurich, Toronto, Chicago, New York City and Boston, Hannaford's Lighthouses on Parade is designed to promote the Greater Portland region and celebrate its artists—while benefiting local charities. And bringing this amazing event to the area required much planning and community support.

In September 2002, a team from Out Front Productions began selling sponsorships for 10- by 4-foot fiberglass lighthouses—and the response was overwhelming! A total of 66 lighthouses were sponsored by businesses, cultural organizations, foundations, civic groups and schools throughout Greater Portland.

Next came the lighthouse design stage. Tim Harrison, President of the American Lighthouse Foundation in Wells, Maine, was consulted for authenticity. Two designs were agreed upon—then sponsors collaborated with local artists including professionals, art teachers and students to bring their lighthouses to life!

Since a main goal of Hannaford's Lighthouses on Parade is to "spark" community pride and spirit—as well as bring smiles to the faces of children and grandparents alike—the assistance of a talented advisory group was also recruited. Members from local non-profit organizations, the City of Portland and the Greater Portland Chambers of Commerce all contributed to make the region's first and only public art display of lighthouses a huge success!

The works of art featured in Hannaford's Lighthouses on Parade first went on display throughout the Greater Portland region in May 2003. In the fall of the same year, they will be auctioned off with 50% of the proceeds going to many local not-for-profits including Maine Center on Deafness, The Senator George J. Mitchell Scholarship Research Institute and the Cancer Community Center. The remaining 50% of the proceeds will be donated to the winning bidder's charity of choice.

For more information about bringing a community art project like Hannaford's Lighthouses on Parade to your community, please contact Out Front Productions at www.thebigparade.com.

Detail from "Art Lights Up Our Lives (ALUOL)"

Detail from "Reunion"

GREATER PORTLAND WELCOMES LIGHTHOUSES ON PARADE

Chambers of Commerce

"Portland is a city of historic charm and new technology, with a proud past and a bright future."
This opening sentence from former U.S. Senator George J. Mitchell's introduction to our book, Portland: Spirit of the
Eastern Seaboard, could not be more accurate. The Portland area is widely regarded as one of the best places to live in
America. And with good reason.

The Greater Portland Chambers of Commerce is pleased to showcase all that our beautiful region has to offer during
Hannaford's Lighthouses on Parade. We hope that while you're here, you'll take the opportunity to stroll our
cobblestone streets, explore our art galleries, walk along our vibrant waterfront, sit down to a lobster feast and,
of course, visit our historic lighthouses. In Portland and our surrounding communities, you'll find a kaleidoscope of
exciting cultural attractions, restaurants, professional sports, entertainment and so much more!

Everywhere you go in and around the Portland area, you'll also be greeted by friendly, outgoing people who call this
wonderful place home. People who live in, work in and contribute to our community—where there's a tremendous
amount of spirit and giving back. It's part of our culture and way of life.

All of us at the Greater Portland Chambers of Commerce extend our appreciation and accolades to Hannaford for
bringing Lighthouses on Parade to Greater Portland. It's a powerful vehicle that will make a difference in the lives of
our citizens. And one that will promote area artists and businesses, support local charities, delight visitors...and light
the way to a bright future.

Sincerely,

W. Godfrey Wood

Godfrey Wood, CEO
Greater Portland Chambers of Commerce

Office of the Mayor

The City of Portland and our neighboring communities are pleased to welcome Hannaford's Lighthouses on Parade. This project is destined to set a standard of excellence for public art that will captivate our area with its brilliance.

We particularly appreciate the charitable commitment of this project, since its effect will be felt throughout the Portland area for years to come. Hannaford's Lighthouses on Parade will touch the lives of many, benefiting a host of local organizations including Maine Center on Deafness, The Senator George J. Mitchell Scholarship Research Institute, the Cancer Community Center and many others.

As a community, we recognize the importance of Hannaford's Lighthouses on Parade as a high-profile means to showcase our wealth of talented, creative artists and our dedicated local business sponsors. We are glad to join cities like Zurich, Chicago, New York City, Boston and Toronto in presenting a truly unique community art project.

Finally, we express our sincere gratitude to everyone involved in this project. Hannaford's Lighthouses on Parade has increased the enjoyment of our city by tourists and residents alike—and is the highest quality representation of our city.

Special thanks are due to Hannaford for shining a new light on Portland by introducing this wonderful event!

Very truly yours,

James F. Cloutier
Mayor

HANNAFORD SHINES NEW LIGHT ON OUR COMMUNITY

Our Presenting Sponsor

A community is at its best when business, government and non-profits partner and collaborate to raise the bar. At Hannaford, we're always looking for opportunities to support community initiatives. Lighthouses on Parade affords a unique and exciting chance to promote the arts, business and tourism—and to assist the many non-profits that enrich our lives.

As a Maine-based company with strong roots in Portland, Hannaford views Lighthouses on Parade as a way to showcase our beautiful city as well as generate enthusiasm and excitement among businesses and residents alike. In Lighthouses on Parade, Hannaford and local businesses have a vehicle to demonstrate community support in an innovative, creative and non-traditional manner.

At Hannaford, we believe our values distinguish us in the marketplace and make us attractive to the people who shop at our stores, work for our company and invest in our future. Supporting and participating in efforts that contribute to the quality of life in the communities we serve has sustained us for more than a century and is the touchstone for our future growth.

A Beacon of Hope

Support for Hannaford's Lighthouses on Parade makes this community art project possible and helps provide significant funding for not-for-profit organizations in the Greater Portland area

The founding charities are:

Maine Center on Deafness

Maine Center on Deafness (MCD) was founded in 1988 to address the problems that deaf and hard-of-hearing people encounter on a daily basis due to discrimination, ignorance or lack of available services. The primary goal of MCD is to create equal and community involvement opportunities for all of these individuals.

Signing for the deaf and hard of hearing will be provided at all Hannaford's Lighthouses on Parade events.

The Senator George J. Mitchell Scholarship Research Institute

Established in 1999 by Senator George Mitchell, the Mitchell Institute gives an annual college scholarship award to a graduating senior from each of Maine's public high schools. This enables Maine youth to reach as far and as high as their individual talents and willingness allow.

Cancer Community Center

The Cancer Community Center, which opened its doors in October 1998, helps individuals affected by cancer enhance their health and well-being. The Center provides support groups led by trained facilitators, a one-on-one peer support program, exercise and stress management programs, a resource library and educational workshops.

14

In the fall of 2003, all of the lighthouses will shine during the Hannaford's Lighthouses on Parade live auction

This exciting event represents a beacon of hope, with 100% of its proceeds being donated to many local charities.

- 50% will be divided equally among the previously mentioned founding charities
- 50% will go to the highest bidder's charity of choice (any qualified 501(c)3)

A portion of the proceeds from the sale of this book will benefit The American Lighthouse Foundation

The American Lighthouse Foundation (ALF) is a non-profit national lighthouse preservation group. ALF currently has 14 lighthouses, requiring over $1 million dollars in restoration funds, under its auspices. Through its educational programs, ALF hopes to ensure that lighthouse history and preservation will be taught to 5th and 6th graders nationwide. ALF also founded the Museum of Lighthouse History in Wells, Maine, where the public can view its collection of rare artifacts and documents.

For more information about ALF—or how to join in the effort to save
our nation's historic lighthouses—please contact:

P.O. Box 889
Wells, Maine 04090
(207) 646-0245
www.LighthouseFoundation.org

Detail from "Cape Collage Light"

ALONG THE WAY

"It was a totally amazing journey into the world of art and artists"

When I was first approached about photographing fiberglass lighthouses and their individual artists during the design process, I was very intrigued. Then I was told that each lighthouse was 10 feet tall and 4 feet wide! Definitely not the typical measurements of my average subjects. From this moment on, photographing the lighthouses and their talented artists became a wondrous assignment...one I've had the privilege to be a part of!

I hope my photographs on the following pages visually convey the scope of the project that each artist wholeheartedly assumed. To design and paint such a large piece is a monumental task. Some artists needed to be extra creative in simply figuring out how to accommodate these dimensions. Artists lacking tall work spaces resorted to positioning lighthouses on their sides–suspended from the ceiling with ropes and hooks or propped up on sawhorses. The lighthouses were painted this way with artists utilizing a "Michelangelo" vertical perspective. Still others cut their creations into pieces to fiberglass back together upon completion. Never underestimate the power of a creative person!

Ladders quickly became an essential element of an artist's required tools. I also took to climbing when I wanted to include my subjects completely, not wanting to overlook any intricate detail so painstakingly recorded.

The wealth of artistic talent was infinite. I photographed artists from the very first brush stroke to near completion, constantly enthralled with the artistic processes and techniques they employed.

Hopefully I have succeeded in making you feel like you were there, too.
I'm sure you will agree each lighthouse is a unique masterpiece in its own right.

– Pauline M. Dimino

Pauline M. Dimino owns and operates Photography by Pauline, a freelance photography business located at 82 Gilman Street in Portland, Maine 04102. Phone: (207) 799-6440 and e-mail: photobypmd@aol.com.
Photograph of Pauline M. Dimino © Mark Myhaver Photography.

Detail from "Facing Northeast"

OFFICIAL LIGHTHOUSES ON PARADE
PHOTOGRAPHERS

Everyone in New England enjoys and takes pride in our lighthouses—and Lighthouses on Parade is a celebration of these treasures. Lest we forget why these steadfast symbols of America are here. A lighthouse by definition is a tower or lofty structure with a powerful light at the top, usually found at the entrance of a port to serve as a guide to navigators.

The lighthouses in this book pay artistic tribute to their ancestors along the coast of Maine. Yet they fulfill another important role—to benefit a wide range of worthy causes throughout our state.

As photographers and strong supporters of our community, we were delighted to take part in this exciting project. From land, sea and sky, lighthouses have been a part of our visual experience for many years. Although we have never put a number on the lighthouses we have photographed, they always serve as captivating subjects. Lighthouses are so simple...so solid. They stand on our rocky coast against nature and time.

As photographers for Lighthouses on Parade, we have had the great fortune to work with many of Maine's talented artists. Once again we found ourselves in good company for a worthwhile cause.

- Dennis and Diana Griggs

Dennis and Diana Griggs founded Tannery Hill Studios in 1977. Their client list would fill a small book and includes a full range of Maine's most memorable people. Contact Dennis and Diana at: 25 Park Drive, Topsham, Maine 04086. Phone: (207) 725-5689 and e-mail: ths@gwi.net.

Thank You From All of Us

Everyone at Out Front Productions would like to extend our heartfelt appreciation to the people of Portland. You have helped make Hannaford's Lighthouses on Parade—and this beautiful book—possible.

Over the past year, we have had the pleasure of meeting and working with your area's business leaders, charity representatives, talented artists and many other community members—all of whom made us feel at home and treated us with gracious hospitality. We would like to especially thank our advisory council, chaired by Barbara Keefe, who provided us with wonderful ideas and inspiration.

At Out Front Productions, it is our goal to create and oversee community art projects from coast to coast that "spark" community spirit and creativity. These innovative programs promote tourism, pride—and generate hundreds of thousands of dollars for local charities as well as countless smiles!

But we could never accomplish any of this without the support of people like you. Your wonderful community has allowed us to create the "spark" that resulted in a tremendously successful—and enjoyable—parade of lighthouses.

Thank you, Hannaford and Portland, for helping light the way!

Howie Jacobson
Managing Partner

Lauren Dixon
Managing Partner

Our Team

(top to bottom and left to right)
Gretchen Bye
Carla Mancuso
Chelsey Graham
Howie Jacobson
Patty Freeman
Barbara Pierce
Christina Williams
Jessica Savage
Lauren Dixon
Rebecca Norr-Hartman
Lou Ann Benigni-Lynch
Tim Coyne
Jillian Eddinger

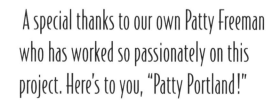

A special thanks to our own Patty Freeman who has worked so passionately on this project. Here's to you, "Patty Portland!"

A Steadfast Symbol
of Our Past

The Guiding Light
for Our Future

$\mathcal{S}$olitude…bravery…beauty…history…strength. These are just a few of the words that are synonymous with the reasons why so many of us are fascinated with lighthouses.

For centuries, these sentinels have been among the oldest standing buildings in America. In fact, there are more stories of bravery, romance and folklore associated with lighthouses than any other structure, a statement that is more evident with the lighthouses of Maine.

Perhaps our love affair with lighthouses began during the mid-nineteenth and twentieth centuries, an era often referred to as the "golden age" of American lighthouses. From that time on, these majestic towers have become an integral part of our daily life.

Since the early days of advertising, many companies have successfully used lighthouses to make a statement that they were "solid," offering customers quality products and honest service. Churches across the country also use lighthouses as a symbol–since, like the church, they were built to save lives.

Lighthouses have inspired poetry, songs and paintings. Artists frequently test their talents by drawing or painting these courageous guardians–and they remain a favorite subject of professional as well as amateur photographers.

Today lighthouses grace license plates, are featured on postage stamps and now appear on the Maine statehood quarter. As their popularity continues to grow, so does our thirst for knowledge about– and quest to preserve–these beautiful symbols of America. Publications about lighthouses are now common, whereas ten years ago, few existed. And in 1994, The American Lighthouse Foundation (ALF) was founded to save not only our historic lighthouses and their artifacts, but the memories of the keepers who lived at them.

Each year, more and more people plan their vacations around and get married at lighthouses. And why not…most are located in breathtaking settings by the sea or in remote tranquil locations. On any day, people are found at lighthouses–relaxing, meditating or falling in love. It's just part of the magic of the lighthouse…a steadfast symbol of our past and the guiding light for our future.

The majestic Portland Head Light is one of the most photographed, recognized and visited lighthouses in the world.

The uniform manual showe where the Lighthouse Depc watchman's badge was to b worn on his hat.

Hat badge of watchmen who guarded the Lighthouse Depot.

One of the most notable wrecks at Portland Head Light occurred when the Annie C. McGuire hit the rocks on Christmas Eve in 1886.

PORTLAND HEAD LIGHT, CASCO BAY, PORTLAND, MAINE.   OLDEST LIGHTHOUSE ON THE COAST.

...AND, MAINE.

106385

Antique postcard showing Portland Head's beam of light shining out into the sea to protect man and vessel.

FIRST KEEPER APPOINTED IN 1791 BY GEORGE WASHINGTON   E-4653

This photograph, taken by the Lubin Moving Picture Company of Philadelphia, was part of a promotion for a movie filmed at Portland Head Light. Shown here (l-r): Assistant keeper John Strout, Mary Strout and keeper Joseph Strout.

When Joshua Strout became keeper of Portland Head Light in 1869, he started a family tradition of lighthouse keeping that would last until the mid 1900s.

Lighthouses often appear on road map covers.

Brass buttons like these were on all uniforms of most employees of the U.S. Lighthouse Service.

Happy Motoring! IN 1960

New England
WITH SPECIAL MAPS OF CITIES

ESSO

The year of this photograph is unknown, but it shows an amazing amount of construction at the Portland Head Light. The back of the photo reads, "To my real friend–Mickey. The most dearly of all, Capt. Strout."

Portland Head Light, Cape Cottage, Me.

Nubble Lighthouse keeper Eugene Coleman, with his beloved lighthouse cat, Sambo Tonkus.

It was this beam of light, as depicted on this antique postcard, that attracted a feast of bugs for Sambo Tonkus to eat.

The railing caps along the outer walkways at Maine's Nubble Lighthouse in York are adorned with miniature brass lighthouses– which are still featured on a number of New England's lighthouses.

Cape Neddick "Nubble" Lighthouse in York is lit up every year from Thanksgiving weekend to January 1st for the holidays–and for one weekend only in the summer months for "Christmas in July."

Image of the new Maine Statehood Quarter, which features Pemaquid Point Lighthouse.

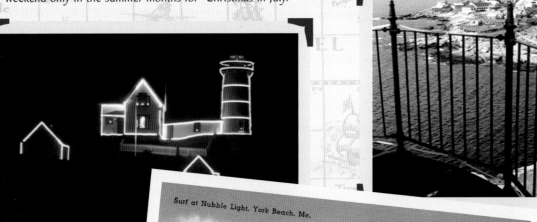

Surf at Nubble Light, York Beach, Me.

Maine's Nubble Light as depicted on this vintage postcard. The house is now painted white, the pyramid bell tower building no longer stands and the little white oil house at water's edge has been painted red for many years.

Located on a small island off Cutler, Little River Lighthouse was draped with an American flag in October of 2001. At this time, after being dark for 26 years, it was relit as a "Beacon of Freedom to the World." In July of 2002, it became the first lighthouse in New England to be transferred to a non-profit group when it was deeded to the American Lighthouse Foundation under the National Historic Lighthouse Preservation Act.

Since the beginning of mass marketing in America, advertising firms used creative images of non-existent lighthouses to promote their products, as did the Franklin Automobile Company from 1902-1934.

This Pemaquid Point postcard dated July of 1912 said on the reverse, "Dear folks, This fog bell has been talking ever since last night when the fog settled down on us."

Pemaquid Point Light, Pemaquid Point, Me.

THE FRANKLIN CAR

FRANKLIN superiority comes from correctness in design; from endurance, efficiency and comfort in service.

The Franklin combination of direct air cooling (no water to boil or freeze), light weight and flexibility gives the greatest safety, ease of control, comfort and economy yet attained in a motor car.

20 miles to the gallon of gasoline.
14,500 miles to the set of tires.
50% slower yearly depreciation.

FRANKLIN AUTOMOBILE COMPANY
SYRACUSE, N. Y.

In April of 1990, Maine's West Quoddy Head Light was one of five lighthouses featured in the Great American Lighthouses postage stamp series issued by the U.S. Postal Service.

The 1839 Saddleback Ledge Light as it appears today.

William Converse Tapley, keeper at Saddleback Ledge Light from 1890-1896.

With food, fresh water and oil running low, a winter storm in 1951 left eighteen-year-old Roger Bruce Williams and two other Coast Guardsmen stranded on Saddleback Ledge for 19 days. With only a day's worth of supplies left, they were finally rescued.

The letter "K," sewn on each side of the jacket lapel, indicated that the individual was the head keeper at a lighthouse—and the number "1" meant that the person was the 1st assistant keeper.

This lady, perhaps one of the keeper's wives, was being hoisted from the lighthouse to an awaiting boat to take her ashore.

June Dudley wrote on this postcard, "Where my Dad was for 10 years." She was referring to her father, Leonard Dudley, who was the keeper at Saddleback Ledge Light in the 1920s.

where my Dad was for 10 year

Pauline Hamor with her beloved Spot, the lighthouse dog of Owls Head Light. Spot was credited for saving the Matinicus mail boat with his bark in the 1930s.

A vintage postcard of Owls Head Light showing the original fog bell tower.

Owl's Head Light off Rockland, Me.

The eggs from the pet chickens of Abbie Burgess, shown here later in life, saved her family from starvation and gave her the strength to keep the lights at the remote Matinicus Rock Lighthouse burning for three weeks.

The twin lights of Matinicus Rock Lighthouse where, thanks to her pet chickens, Abbie Burgess became one of Maine's most famous lighthouse heroines.

Although the Coast Guard maintains the beacon in the tower, the Heron Neck Light Station, as it appears today, is privately owned.

Nemo, the "fog-bark" at Heron Neck Light Station.

Photo of Pauline Hamor and Spot from the collection of Bill Geilfuss.

The Portland Breakwat
Lighthouse as it appea
shortly after it was first
in 1875. The keeper's
house no longer stand

The original Portland Breakwater
Lighthouse (Bug Light) was built in
1855. It was discontinued in 1875 and
replaced by the current tower.

Lighthouse keepers were awarded a red Efficiency
Star for being commended by the Lighthouse
Inspector at their quarterly inspections.

Breakwater Light, Portland Harbor at night, Portland, Maine

This vintage postcard of Portland
Breakwater Lighthouse shows a
six-masted schooner in the harbor.

Lighthouses have long been a
symbol of safety and security.

64499

This book was used by Chance Brothers & Co. of England to sell Fresnel lenses to the U.S. Lighthouse Service.

DESCRIPTION AND PLANS

of

LIGHTS FOR LIGHT

ACCORDING TO THE CATADIOP

of

AUGUSTIN FRES

AND THE

HOLOPHOTAL SYSTEM AND OP

MANUFACTURED BY CHANC

GLASS WORKS, NE

MEDICAL HANDBOOK
UNITED STATES LIGHTHOUSE SERVICE
1915

The U.S. Lighthouse Service manufactured brass lighthouses in various sizes for a wide range of purposes. The largest design was 24 inches high by 15 inches wide at its base.

Since most lighthouses were in remote areas or on islands, the Lighthouse Service published a medical handbook to deal with just about every type of sickness and injury.

Captain Howard T. Ball and his wife Lucy, shown here with three of their nine children, were keepers of Eagle Island Lighthouse from 1898 until Howard's death in 1913.

Eagle Island Lighthouse was automated in 1959. Shortly thereafter, the Coast Guard offered the keeper's house to anyone who agreed to move it. No one accepted this offer–and in 1963, the Coast Guard tore it down and burned the remains. The tower still stands.

Photo of Captain Howard T. Ball, his wife and children courtesy of Norma Ball Gray.

Marcus A. Hanna, a Civil War Medal of Honor recipient, served as keeper at Cape Elizabeth Lights in the late 1800s. In 1885, he was awarded the gold life saving medal for his almost impossible rescue of crew members of the vessel Australia. However, he was unable to save the life of the captain.

The Cape Elizabeth west tower as it appears today. During World War II, it was used as a lookout post to watch for enemy vessels.

This vintage postcard from the early 1900s shows how powerful the beams of light were at Cape Elizabeth's twin lighthouses.

The official logo of the U.S. Department of Commerce approved in the 1930s.

TWO LIGHTS BY NIGHT CAPE ELIZABETH MAINE

From a 1920s painting by Edward Hopper, Cape Elizabeth became the first lighthouse to appear on a U.S. Postage stamp in 1970.

MAINE STATEHOOD
1820-1970
U.S. POSTAGE SIX CENTS

PORTLAND
JULY
9
1970
ME

FIRST DAY OF ISSUE

West Light.

East Light.

PORTLAND LIGHTS. FIRST LIGHTS SEEN, COMING TO PORTLAND.

An image of both the west and east towers at Cape Elizabeth Lighthouse is shown in this 1904 vintage postcard.

The official flag of the U.S. Lighthouse Service. In the 1920s, the Lighthouse Inspector awarded it to Cape Elizabeth lighthouse keeper, Frank Cotton, for having the best-run lighthouse station in the First Lighthouse District.

Beginning in 1941, civilian employees of the U.S. Coast Guard who were associated with lighthouses wore this style of hat emblem.

The first issue of Lighthouse Digest in May of 1992 was newspaper in style and only 16 pages long. Proving the popularity of lighthouses, the magazine currently has subscribers in all 50 states and 17 countries.

LIGHTHOUSE DIGEST

COMPLIMENTARY ISSUE

MAY 1992

Massachusetts Developer to Save Historic Light Station

HERON NECK RESCUE

One of the biggest uproars in lighthouse preservation history is drawing to a close with the Coast Guard's announcement that it has picked a lessee for historic and fire damaged Heron Neck Light Station.

In what gained national attention from nearly every newspaper in the United States and the NBC Today Show, a nearly 2 year bureaucratic nightmare will come to a close and a new happier beginning for everyone concerned.

It has been nearly 3 years since an electrical fire destroyed part of the keeper's quarters at Heron Neck Lighthouse which sits majestically atop a cliff of sand colored granite on Greens Island southwest of Carvers Harbor near Vinalhaven Maine.

Heron Neck, built in 1854 and on the National List of Historic Places, is a picture perfect post card location, except for the gaping hole in the roof caused by the fire which has left the building exposed to the elements and deterioration.

The Coast Guard, which is not in the business of maintaining obsolete structures, had assembled a demolition crew to tear down the damaged structure when preservation groups came forward and asked for a reprieve. The Coast Guard agreed that it would lease the buildings out, but it took over 2 years of red tape to finally decide who would actually be awarded the lease.

The lease has been awarded to Charles Whitten, a Massachusetts developer who has experience in restoration having restored a 95 year old lifesaving station in Damariscove Island Maine.

Peter Ralston of the Island Institute in Rockland Maine who was instrumental in saving Heron Neck from the wrecker's ball is quoted as saying

continued under Heron page 2

The 1828 Cape Elizabeth east tower was painted with red stripes in 1865. The tower was torn down in 1874 and replaced with one that stands in the same location today.

Detail from "Lighting Liberty"

94.9 WHOM Lighthouse

Sponsor:
Citadel Broadcasting 94.9 WHOM

Artist:
Melani Darrell, Art Works by Melani

For the past 45 years, 94.9 WHOM has been broadcasting from the top of Mt. Washington. Delivering the largest geographic coverage area of any FM radio station in North America, 94.9 WHOM features a light rock format that appeals to listeners ages 35-64 in five states and parts of Canada. 94.9 WHOM sees Lighthouses on Parade as a unique way to promote the station to people living in Maine—as well as to tourists visiting this beautiful area.

"94.9 WHOM Lighthouse" provides a breathtaking view of the station's entire coverage area from the peak of Mt. Washington. Creating it enabled well-known local artist, Melani Darrell, to depart from her coastal themes and share her deep love for the high forests of the northeast. In addition to mountains, the delightful "journey of imagery" incorporates water, trees, animals and plant life—all resulting in a powerful yet tranquil design.

Sponsor:
HP Hood Inc.

Artist:
Toni Wolf

As New England's leading dairy manufacturer—with a long-standing tradition of serving the community—HP Hood is pleased to participate in Lighthouses on Parade. Founded in 1846, HP Hood is currently one of the largest branded dairy operators in the United States. The dairy produces a variety of products including milk, cultured foods, citrus beverages, extended-shelf-life dairy, frozen desserts, non-dairy and specialty drinks.

"A Colorful ChildHOOD," created by Toni Wolf, a self-employed artist, pays tribute to the Children's Museum of Maine. Designed to look like a page from a coloring book, this whimsical lighthouse features realistic crayons, the HP Hood blimp floating in the sky and a kite that represents the Children's Museum of Maine logo.

A Light for All Seasons

Sponsor:
Brigham's Ice Cream

Artist:
Susan Arsenault

Many generations have grown up enjoying the delicious ice cream and sundae concoctions found only at Brigham's Ice Cream parlors. Founded in downtown Boston in 1914, Brigham's is a household name in the Greater Boston area—and today its ice creams and yogurts are also available in supermarkets. In fact, Brigham's Vanilla Ice Cream quart is the #1 selling frozen food in Boston!

Brigham's participates in many Boston-area fundraising events—and welcomed the opportunity to support the Portland community by sponsoring "A Light for All Seasons." Designed by Susan Arsenault, artist and avid lighthouse fan, it depicts a tree and its surroundings on the coast of Maine. As each of the four seasons meld into the next, a spectacular array of color comes to life.

A Twilight Winter Odyssey

Sponsor:
Time Warner Cable of Maine

Artists:
Employees and family members of Time Warner Cable of Maine

Time Warner Cable of Maine is proud to be a part of the Greater Portland community and support local charities. As a leading provider of information and home entertainment, Time Warner Cable of Maine enhances its products and services to provide customers with more choice and the greatest value.

"A Twilight Winter Odyssey" showcases Maine's natural splendor. Staff and family members from Time Warner Cable of Maine, assisted by Heidi Klelber, Pam Buswell, Deb Gillespie, Cheryl Tait, Kathy Doten and Catalina Mehler, used acrylic paints to create a twilight setting of peace, tranquility and breathtaking beauty.

Artists Led By:
Heidi Klelber, Pam Buswell, Deb Gillespie, Cheryl Tait, Kathy Doten and Catalina Mehler

Aesop's Light

Sponsor:
The Museum of Glass & Ceramics

Artist:
Brita Holmquist,
The Jameson Gallery

The Museum of Glass & Ceramics features a world-class collection of over 12,000 quality objects including blown, cut and pressed glass, wheel-thrown to coil-built pottery, earthenware and porcelain ceramics. The museum is expanding—and is scheduled to open a new location in 2005. In fact, its future site has served as the "home base" for the Lighthouses on Parade works of art.

"Aesop's Light," designed by Brita Holmquist, a professional painter in Maine for 30 years, is based on one of Aesop's best-loved fables. An extremely thirsty crow flew to a pitcher she saw in a window. But no matter how hard she tried, the water was too low for the crow to reach. At last, seeing pebbles lying nearby, she placed them one by one in the pitcher until the water level reached the brim. Finally the crow could drink her fill. The symbolic moral of the story: What we cannot do by force, we can accomplish by work and invention.

Lighthouse Donated By:
R. Bonechi Imports

Special Thanks To:
Upscale Consignment Furniture, Inc.
for artist's work space and Adam's Glass

Sponsor:
WMTW Broadcast Group

Artist:
Bob Jordan

WMTW Broadcast Group, LLC, located in Portland's Monument Square, consists of ABC 8 WMTW; News Radio WMTW 870, 1470 AM and 106.7 FM; WTHT 107.5 FM "The Wolf"; WMEK 99.9 FM "Kiss 99.9" and wmtw.com.

"Airwaves" was designed by freelance artist Bob Jordan, along with a group of his friends who assisted with painting. This lighthouse conveys the many entities of WMTW Broadcast Group—creating a mosaic of energy through music, news, sports, entertainment and community involvement.

ART LIGHTS UP OUR LIVES (ALUOL)

Sponsor:
The House of Lights

Artists:
Students from Skillin Elementary
School in South Portland

As a leading retail lighting showroom, The House of Lights is excited about this opportunity to shine a new light on the Portland community and its charities! Established in 1955, The House of Lights sells light fixtures, table and floor lamps, bulbs and accessories to homeowners, contractors, designers and architects.

Approximately 400 K-5 students from Skillin Elementary School participated in designing and decorating "Art Lights Up Our Lives." Assisted by art teachers Susan Cox and Heather Libby, the children used a mix of acrylic paint and découpage to create self-portraits and original artwork for this unique lighthouse.

Student Artists Directed By:
Art teacher Susan Cox and student teacher Heather Libby

Right Page: Detail from "Art Lights Up Our Lives"

BAYLIGHT

Sponsor:
RE/MAX By The Bay

Artists:
Maylynn Philbrick, aMayzing by Design and Lucas Montague

In 2002, RE/MAX By The Bay, whose motto is "Always Exceeding Your Expectations," was voted the #1 real estate office in Maine. As a community leader, RE/MAX By The Bay takes great pride in supporting Maine charities and the artistic culture of Portland. This wonderful community art project will bring a smile to everyone who joins the parade!

"Baylight" is a reflection of the community RE/MAX By The Bay's 50 brokers love—and watch grow—from their home on Baxter Boulevard. A collaborative effort between Maylynn Philbrick and Lucas Montague, this lighthouse features scenes of the Back Bay at sunset, colors of the changing seasons, hot air balloons in flight and shining stars. "Baylight" is powered by three solar panels and has interior mirrors to help redirect and magnify light.

Special Thanks To:
Dave Libby from Communications Facilities, Inc.
for donating a warm space for the artists to paint!

Sponsor:
Women In Need, Inc. (WINI)

Artist:
Rachel Michaud

In addition to being a fun-filled community event, Women In Need, Inc. (WINI) believes Lighthouses on Parade matches its mission. As a beacon for women in transition, refugees and immigrants living in the Greater Portland area, WINI offers women from diverse backgrounds and cultures a wide variety of programs, training and consultation to help them adjust to life in America.

WINI envisions a future Maine that takes pride in and cherishes its rich diversity of nationalities and races, giving "Beacon of Celebration & Unity" significant meaning. Designed by Rachel Michaud, this captivating lighthouse features the Portland skyline, harbor and figures representing five continents. It serves as WINI's tribute to women of all races and cultures in Portland—and celebrates their continued contributions to the state of Maine.

Lighthouse Donated By:
Bully Hill Winery
The Official Wine of Lighthouses on Parade

BEACON OF LIGHT

Sponsor:
Verrill & Dana, LLP

Artists:
The families and volunteers of
The Center for Grieving Children

Verrill & Dana, LLP, which has long been one of Maine's most prominent and respected law firms, is proud to be partnering with The Center for Grieving Children on this important community project.

For over 15 years, The Center for Grieving Children has provided a safe haven for children and family members dealing with grief related to bereavement and life-threatening illnesses. "Beacon of Light," which is modeled after The Center's Memorial Star Wall, reflects The Center's vision to "be a beacon of light in the hearts and souls of grieving children throughout the world." The colors portray a night sky with golden stars, each one created by a family at The Center.

BLUE WILLOW TEAPARTY

Sponsor:
The Shops at Clark's Pond

Artist:
Greta Bank

The Shops at Clark's Pond, owned and managed by a Chicago-based company that marveled at the success of the original Cows on Parade, is excited about the impact Lighthouses on Parade will have on this area! A community shopping center located in South Portland, The Shops at Clark's Pond is anchored by Craft-Mania, HomeGoods, Hoyt's Cinema, Marshalls, Decathlon USA Sports Megastore, Olive Garden, T.G.I. Fridays and more than 20 other great shops and services.

Local artist Greta Bank designed "Blue Willow Teaparty," a charming interpretation of the centuries-old Blue Willow pattern found on porcelain and earthenware dishes. Originally based on an ancient Chinese fable about eternal love, the pattern was later modified by English craftsmen. This whimsical teapot is a tribute to our American history—as well as to the popular pattern that's still highly collectible.

CAPE APE

Sponsor:
Harbour Lights

Artists:
Jay Piscopo and David Roberts

As pioneers in the lighthouse giftware industry, Harbour Lights simply had to participate in this wonderful community art event! Harbour Lights is the preeminent manufacturer of authentic, detailed lighthouse replicas—and has produced numerous award-winning models since 1991. With the added focus on lighthouse preservation, Harbour Lights is proud to help protect our nation's historic sentinels.

"Cape Ape" was created by freelance artist and cartoonist Jay Piscopo, assisted by David Roberts, a local commercial artist and Web designer. This captivating lighthouse is purposely designed to resemble a Harbour Lights miniature—only on a much larger scale! It also pays homage to classic monster movies. A giant gorilla, constructed of a steel frame, Styrofoam and papier-maché, sits atop the lighthouse. With an airplane in its grasp, this gorilla proves that it's king of the lighthouse parade!

Sponsor:
City of Portland

Artist:
Scott Potter

Recently named the #1 place in the country to raise children, Portland is a city of vast opportunity. It holds a key place in a business corridor extending from New York to Atlantic Canada, yet offers a welcome relief from big-city life. Portland also supports a vibrant community of visual and performing arts. Whether planning to vacation in or relocate to Portland, this enterprising, progressive and livable city will exceed your expectations in ways you never imagined!

Scott Potter, an internationally acclaimed designer known for elegant servingware and decorative accessories, created "Cape Collage Light." It was inspired by the classic early European prints and gold colorations that are the hallmark of Scott's artwork and découpage. This enchanting lighthouse features various prints of sea life from around the globe. All papers used were hand-cut, then applied with adhesives and sealed.

Children – Lighting Up the Future

Sponsor:
Law Offices of Joe Bornstein

Artist:
Susan J. York

For over 28 years, the Law Offices of Joe Bornstein has represented the interests of low- to moderate-income Maine residents. Many of these people are unemployed or disabled. As a personal injury law firm that takes pride in the community, the Law Offices of Joe Bornstein is pleased to give back to the Greater Portland area in this civic and philanthropic way.

"Children – Lighting Up the Future" was designed by Susan J. York, a passionate storyteller who frequently uses art to bring stories to life. Camille Davidson, students from the Levey Day School and the poem "I'd Like to Be a Lighthouse" by Rachel Lyman Field, also provided inspiration for this lighthouse. It features seven children who represent a menorah, a girl reaching for a star, an evening sky filled with Stars of David and biblical quotes.

Special Thanks To:
Adam Nichols, a senior at Southern Aroostook Vocational Education, his classmates and teacher Amy Toby, for applying the topcoat and transporting this lighthouse

Right Page: Detail from "The House of Stone and Light"

www.headlightav.com

Sponsor:
Headlight Audio Visual, Inc.

Artists:
Don and Betsey Wright, The Signery

Headlight Audio Visual, Inc. couldn't miss this opportunity to help local charities while promoting its company's capabilities. Owned and operated by Robert Bruns since 1975, Headlight Audio Visual has evolved into the premier audio/visual company in Maine. In addition to specializing in the sale, rental and installation of equipment, Headlight Audio Visual offers videoconferencing, duplication services, production, equipment service and event consultation.

"Coming Home" represents different classes of ships that rely on lighthouses to safely guide them through global waters every day—just as customers depend on Headlight Audio Visual to help them navigate in the complex world of audio/visual equipment. Don and Betsey Wright, owners of The Signery, Maine's most complete and creative signage resource, designed this intriguing lighthouse.

Sponsor:
Barber Foods

Artists:
Valerie Betts and Maureen Magee,
Sow's Ear Studio

Since opening its doors in 1955, family-owned and operated Barber Foods has been serving the Greater Portland area and beyond. As a leading manufacturer and marketer of specialty chicken products, Barber Foods saw Lighthouses on Parade as a natural extension to serve and support the community.

Created by artists Valerie Betts and Maureen Magee, "Dinner Is Served" replicates a 1950s-style kitchen. The mid-winter scene illustrates that Barber Foods are distributed frozen—and the table is set for a delicious chicken dinner. Outside, a dark winter sky is reflected on the lighthouse lens. Patches of snow adorn stone steps, trees and the mailbox. The family cat, also welcome at the dinner table, is even warmed by a colorful scarf!

FACES OF MAINE

Sponsor:
Hannaford Bros. Co.

Presenting Sponsor
for Lighthouses on Parade

Artists:
King Middle School's Project S.A.F.E. and S.M.A.R.T. art club, directed by Melissa Prescott

Hannaford Bros. Co. is proud to bring Lighthouses on Parade to the Portland community. As our business grows at Hannaford, we will continue to build on the foundation and values that have sustained our company for more than a century. We will also continue to support efforts—like this community art project—that contribute to the quality of life in the communities we serve.

"Faces of Maine," created by King Middle School's art club students under the direction of Melissa Prescott, collectively merges many ideas into one successful piece of art. Every student contributed to the design of friendly faces, using acrylic paints to create smaller images that are laminated onto the surface of this lighthouse.

Sponsor:
Maine Center on Deafness

Artists:
Brenda Schertz, Guillaume Chastel, Margaret Chastel and Julie Novack

Maine Center on Deafness (MCD) was founded in 1988 to address discrimination against deaf and hard-of-hearing people. MCD provides information, empowerment, advocacy and referral services to these individuals—and believes Lighthouses on Parade will play an important role in promoting public awareness of the community's deaf culture as well as the Maine Telecommunications Relay Service.

A collage of old and new photographs, "FaceTs of Communication" showcases the many ways the hearing and deaf communicate. Created by freelance artists Brenda Schertz, Guillaume Chastel, Margaret Chastel and Julie Novack, this lighthouse design incorporates images of deaf people, sign language, facial expressions and other means of communication.

Underwritten By:
AT&T

FACING NORTHEAST

Sponsor:
Northeast Bank

Artists:
Northeast Bank Employees,
directed by Tim Schwab,
Cottonschwab Creative Unlimited

Northeast Bank, a Maine-based financial institution with 13 locations throughout the state, prides itself on delivering the best products, friendly service and expert advice to meet specific consumer and business needs. Northeast Bank feels Lighthouses on Parade is an ideal way to support the community—and thank employees, family members and customers.

"Facing Northeast," designed by Northeast Bank staff—along with Tim Schwab, known for his diverse creative services ranging from photography to Web design—features a collage of thousands of photographs. From a distance, the intriguing mix of laser prints, duo-tones and découpage form a magnificent view of Maine's shoreline. Upon closer inspection, images of faces representing the people of Maine are revealed.

Sponsor:
The Eastland Park Hotel

Artist:
Dave G. Hall

The Eastland Park Hotel, a historic landmark located in the acclaimed arts district of Portland, is supportive of cultural community efforts—especially those that benefit worthy causes. Since opening its doors in 1927, The Eastland Park Hotel has been referred to as Portland's First Lady of Hospitality. The 202-room hotel recently went through renovations, restoring its traditional rich appearance and adding amenities for the modern traveler. An elegant ballroom with balcony and marbled step entrance hosts many of the hotel's wonderful events and brings to life its tagline, "A Glorious Past. A Magnificent Future."

"First Lady" is a miniature replica of The Eastland Park Hotel. Designed by Dave G. Hall—an elementary art teacher and painter represented by several galleries throughout the state of Maine—this lighthouse creatively depicts the elegance and ambience of the grand historic hotel that is a beacon of the community.

Sponsor:
Portland Press Herald/ Maine Sunday Telegram

Official Media Partner for Lighthouses on Parade

Artists:
Cheryl Dobson and Jane Fortune

The Portland Press Herald/Maine Sunday Telegram, Maine's leading newspaper, welcomes the opportunity to be part of this large-scale community art project! Publishing since 1862, the newspaper has earned a nationwide reputation for top-quality journalism, exceptional printing, design and commitment to the communities it serves.

Appropriately named "Front Page," this lighthouse features a collage of front pages and special sections that have appeared in the Portland Press Herald/Maine Sunday Telegram. Its design highlights the overall mission of the newspaper—and positions it as the source for news and information customers trust and value. Artists Cheryl Dobson and Jane Fortune, who teamed up to be creative and have fun, also used mirror tile to reflect light—and illustrate how the newspaper is a reflection of the community.

Right Page: Detail from "The Right Direction"

Sponsor:
Portland Pirates

Artist:
Tatia DiChiara

In Portland, hockey is a sport that is unsurpassed in popularity. And the Portland Pirates have been bringing American Hockey League excitement to the city for 25 years! The team, which is affiliated with the National Hockey League's Washington Capitals, is also committed to helping several area non-profit organizations throughout the 2003 season—and is pleased to help the designated Lighthouses on Parade charities reach their goals!

"The Goalkeeper," created by artist Tatia DiChiara, depicts hockey's last line of defense in a compelling way. A native of Maine who recently moved back to the area, Tatia teamed up with her father and engineer, William Squiers, to shape, sculpt and attach goalie's arms to this lighthouse. It was then sanded, sprayed with automotive primer and painted with acrylic enamel. An official team jersey, goalie pads, stick and helmet with blinking light top off this lighthouse that's ready for action—on and off the ice!

Engineer:
William Squiers

Sponsor:
Hannaford Bros. Co.

Presenting Sponsor for Lighthouses on Parade

Artist:
Diane Bragdon

As the presenting sponsor of Lighthouses on Parade, Hannaford Bros. Co. is extremely excited to support the Portland community and its artists. Established in 1883 by Arthur Hannaford—who was later joined by his brothers, Howard and Edward—the company still operates under its founding principle: Deliver the highest quality products at the fairest prices. Today Hannaford has 119 supermarkets and food and drug stores in Maine, New Hampshire, Vermont, New York and Massachusetts.

Created by Diane Bragdon, a full-time Hannaford associate, "Hannaford Headlight" celebrates the historic lighthouses of Maine. A local artist specializing in landscape and seascape paintings and prints, Diane has found that Maine's natural surroundings are full of composition and unlimited design possibilities.

HAVEN'S LIGHT

Sponsor:
Haven's Candies
Official Confectioner of Lighthouses on Parade

Artist:
Dave G. Hall

With a long history of supporting local charities, it was a natural fit for Haven's Candies to join in the Lighthouses on Parade project! Since 1915, Haven's Candies has been handcrafting premium confections, using timeless recipes and only the finest ingredients. The store's chocolates, fudges, salt-water taffy, roasted nuts and chocolate novelties have delighted candy lovers for generations. Stop by any Haven's Candies location during your visit to Lighthouses on Parade to sample a sweet treat!

Created by art teacher and artist Dave G. Hall, "Haven's Light" is designed to portray candy throughout the seasons—from Christmas to Easter. This lighthouse features Plexiglas windows airbrushed to look as if it's full of jelly beans, large handmade "chocolates" that circle the base and "candies" that are cast, constructed or painted onto the surface. We're sure you'll agree that this colorful lighthouse looks good enough to eat!

Sponsor:
Gifford's Famous Ice Cream

Artist:
Thomas K. Merriam

For over four generations, family-owned Gifford's Famous Ice Cream has operated Dairy Bars in Maine and distributed its products throughout New England and surrounding areas. Old family recipes, fresh local milk and cream, the highest quality ingredients—along with ripples and flavorings—all combine to make Gifford's ice cream so delicious!

As a supporter of the arts, Gifford's wanted to create a lighthouse that portrayed its passion for ice cream in a fun and idyllic way. Thomas K. Merriam, an accomplished cartoonist specializing in carved and illustrated signs, was the perfect choice for "Heaven's Light." Constructed from high-density sign foam, chromatic sign paints and auto body filler, this lighthouse captures the good times and spirit of those who simply love ice cream. Sitting down with a scoop of your favorite flavor is truly "heaven!"

Sponsor:
Kennebunk Savings Bank

Artist:
Robert Dohar

Kennebunk Savings Bank is delighted to sponsor "Highlights of York County," which showcases the beautiful natural resources in this unique community! As York County's leading community bank, Kennebunk Savings Bank—together with its subsidiary, Morris Insurance Services, Inc.—is committed to serving the financial needs of both individuals and businesses. Each year, the bank also contributes 10% of its earnings back to non-profits and charitable organizations in York County—making the area a better place to live, work and do business.

Robert Dohar, an illustrator working primarily out of New York City as well as in southern Maine, shares Kennebunk Savings Bank's joy for York County. He used high-quality oil paint over primer on "Highlights of York County" to magnificently capture the sights of this breathtaking community.

THE HOUSE OF STONE AND LIGHT

Sponsor:
Portland Arts and Technology
High School (PATHS)

Artists:
Diane Manzi and
commercial art class students

Portland Arts and Technology High School serves 23 different school districts in southern Maine. Because PATHS is a school of choice, a unique atmosphere exists. A climate based on mutual respect, caring and high expectations permeates the facility.

"The House of Stone and Light" is a multi-media piece embellished by PATHS' commercial art class students. Led by art instructor Diane Manzi, every student played a role in creating this intriguing lighthouse. Painted to look like stone and glass, it features mosaic windows, mirrors, a slate-like roof, organic shapes and gold-leaf accents.

Special Thanks To:
An anonymous lighthouse donor who made it possible for PATHS to contribute to the Greater Portland community

67

In the Limelight

Sponsor:
Portland Stage Company

Artists:
Anita Stewart, Jacqueline Firkins, Ted Gallant and Heather Hutton

As Maine's premier professional theatre and the state's only full member of the national League of Resident Theatres (LORT), Portland Stage Company demonstrates a commitment to the highest standards. Since its founding in 1974 as The Profile Theatre, Portland Stage Company has been a cornerstone of Portland's arts scene. It engages, entertains and educates an annual audience of more than 40,000 area residents and nearly 7,000 students with classic, contemporary and new works.

"In the Limelight" brings the stage to the streets of Portland. Anita Stewart, Jacqueline Firkins, Ted Gallant and Heather Hutton—artists and craftspeople who design and build sets and costumes for Portland Stage Company—constructed this lighthouse. After cutting it in half, the artists used Styrofoam, multi-colored and textured fabrics plus Plexiglas windows to create drama. Take a peek inside the windows...and enchanting characters dressed in period costumes will entertain you!

Right Page: Detail from "In the Limelight"

Sponsor:
Skillful Vending

Artists:
Over 3,200
Portland public school students

Skillful Vending is proud to salute Portland and its magnificent lighthouses that shine a guiding light to welcome people from around the world. A family business celebrating its 25th anniversary, Skillful Vending provides entertainment and great times for the people of Maine...just for the fun of it!

With multicolored mosaic tiles woven throughout most of its design, "Just for the FUN of It" was created by K-5 Portland public school children under the direction of their art teachers. Upon closer inspection, each tile displays a happy self-portrait of a student. The overall theme of this lighthouse represents some of the wonderful—and magical—entertainment that Skillful Vending offers.

Student Artists Directed By:

Sally W. Rodstrom, Kathie Porensky, Bob Auclair, Ellen Handleman, Maryjane Johnston, Peg Richard, Pat Reed, Ed Perry, Sherman Kendall, Terry Therrien, Jessica Goudreau, Steve Rodstrom and Ross and Jennifer Furman

Special Thanks To:

Meryl and Barbara Hallett for providing studio space

Sponsor:
DiMillo's Floating Restaurant

Artists:
Mark Edward Drew and John Charles Angelopoulos, 'm'archangel'

Welcome aboard! Since 1982, family-owned and operated DiMillo's Floating Restaurant has been serving exceptional seafood as well as American and Italian cuisine. Founded by the late Tony DiMillo, this nationally famous restaurant was originally an old car ferry named the Newport. It really is afloat— and at low tide, rests on 12 feet of Portland Harbor water.

Designed by Mark Edward Drew and John Charles Angelopoulos, co-owners of 'm'archangel', "King Crustacean" is a tribute to the most delicious shellfish served at DiMillo's—the Maine lobster. Acrylic paints, as well as several trompe l'oeil and cartoon techniques, were used to create this larger-than-life lobster that challenges the throne of King Kong!

Sponsor:
Choice One Communications

Official Web Developer for Lighthouses on Parade

Artists:
Students from the School at Sweetser

Headquartered in Rochester, New York, Choice One Communications Inc. is a leading integrated communications services provider. The company offers voice and data services, including Internet and DSL solutions, plus Web hosting and design. Choice One currently services small- to medium-sized businesses in 29 markets throughout the northeast and midwest.

"Ladders of Hope" was designed by students from the School at Sweetser, directed by art teachers Lisa Trembly and Robin Pietila. To celebrate the School at Sweetser's 175th anniversary, the students chose to create an image that symbolizes the vision of the organization—helping people find promising futures. This engaging lighthouse features a group of people assisting one another up a ladder toward their goals.

Student Artists Directed By:
Art teachers Lisa Trembly and Robin Pietila

Right Page: Detail from "Ladders of Hope"

LIGHT COMMENTARY

Sponsor:
Saco Spirit, Inc.
Saco, Maine—
A Main Street Maine Community

Artists:
Thornton Academy art club students

Saco Spirit, Inc. is proud to showcase the talented students from Thornton Academy and help benefit the community! As a non-profit organization, Saco Spirit strives to make Saco a better place to live and work by enhancing the vitality of the downtown area.

Created by Thornton Academy art club students, assisted by Jennifer Merry, Christine Prosser and Mike Theriault, "Light Commentary" features dozens of quotations stenciled in various type styles. Each inspirational message relates to education, thought, light and life. A cubist design, geometric shapes and fragmented colors add to this lighthouse's intrigue.

Student Artists Directed By:
Jennifer Merry, Christine Prosser and student intern Mike Theriault

Sponsor:
Cancer Community Center

Artist:
James A. Taliana

Founded in 1998, Cancer Community Center supports and promotes the well-being of cancer patients and their families. Its programs, offered free of charge in comfortable settings where special bonds develop, include one-on-one and group support, wellness events and creative expression workshops.

"The Light of Life," designed by full-time artist and gallery owner James A. Taliana, truly represents the spirit of community and support found at the Cancer Community Center. An image of people joining hands and encircling a tree of life is repeated on all sides of this lighthouse. Colorful latex paints bring the colors of the four seasons to life, symbolizing hope for the future.

LIGHT OF THE BUMBLE BEE

Sponsors:
Nappi Distributors and High Falls Brewing Company

Artist:
Diane Bragdon

Nappi Distributors and High Falls Brewing Company are pleased to support the Greater Portland community by participating in this high-profile, fun-filled program. Located in Portland, Nappi Distributors is a multi-generation beer, wine and non-alcoholic beverage wholesaler. J.W. Dundee Honey Brown is one of the popular beer products the company sells.

High Falls Brewing Company, based in Rochester, New York, is currently in the third year of operation under its new name. The company is celebrating the 125th Anniversary of Genesee Beer and the eighth year of J.W. Dundee Honey Brown. Since it was the presenting sponsor of Horses on Parade in Rochester, High Falls Brewing Company is extremely excited to be a part of Lighthouses on Parade!

"Light of the Bumble Bee" was created by local artist Diane Bragdon. The playful design is beehive-themed to tie in with Honey Brown Beer's "Honey Bee" logo. Diane's creativeness has resulted in an appealing, fun and exciting production that will have everyone buzzing!

Sponsor:
Unum Provident Corporation

Artists:
Mark Edward Drew and
John Charles Angelopoulos,
'm'archangel'

With a long history of supporting the arts in Greater Portland, Unum Provident Corporation believes art plays an integral and vital role in our community. Unum Provident is the world leader in protecting income and lifestyles through its comprehensive offering of group, individual and voluntary benefits, products and services. The company has operations in the United States, Canada and the United Kingdom.

"Lighting Liberty," created by Mark Edward Drew and John Charles Angelopoulos, co-owners of 'm'archangel', depicts candle bearers ascending lighthouse stairs to maintain the beacon of Liberty. The artists used acrylic paints and set design techniques for this lighthouse's figures and stone facade.

Sponsor:
Pape Chevrolet, Inc.

Artist:
Melani Darrell, Art Works by Melani

Pape Chevrolet has long been a supporter of several charities in central and southern Maine—and is pleased to be a part of Lighthouses on Parade! Founded in 1967 by Fred Pape, Jr., the Chevrolet dealership has since added Mitsubishi and Hummer to its line. In 2002, market area surveys ranked Pape Chevrolet as "The best of the best car dealerships to do business with."

Each year, people from around the world come to see the historic lighthouses of Portland-area harbors, which are beautifully illustrated on "The Lights of Casco Bay." When using acrylic paints to create this lighthouse, artist Melani Darrell wanted to give viewers a different perspective from all sides. And even though the featured lighthouses are not exact duplications, they provide a lasting impression of Maine's well-known icons.

Sponsor:
FleetBoston Financial

Artists:
Chet S. Wancewicz and
Johanna F. Hoffman

FleetBoston Financial is the seventh-largest financial holding company in the United States. Its principal businesses, Personal Financial Services and Wholesale Banking, offer a comprehensive array of innovative financial solutions to 20 million customers. Fleet carries on a long legacy of civic leadership, community service and enduring partnerships in the communities it serves. The company supports programs in Maine that focus on K-12 public education, economic opportunity and youth development as well as arts and culture.

"The Lights of Maine" was created by retired teacher and artist Chet S. Wancewicz and Johanna F. Hoffman, a freelance illustrator, restoration specialist and professional picture framer. A tribute to the sentinels that dot the coast, "The Lights of Maine" features 63 lighthouse images, mirrors, shells, lobster designs and a poem about the guardians of the sea. Over 300 hours, 16 days and a mix of acrylic paints combined with lots of love to bring this magnificent lighthouse to life.

MAINE'S BRIGHTEST LIGHT

Sponsor:
The Senator George J. Mitchell Scholarship Research Institute

Artist:
Melani Darrell, Art Works by Melani

Lighthouses on Parade is a wonderful opportunity to participate in a worthy community effort while increasing awareness of the Mitchell Scholarship Program. Striving to create educational opportunities for Maine's youth, The Mitchell Institute awards annual scholarships to graduating students from every public high school in the state. Scholarships are based on academic promise, community service and financial need.

"Maine's Brightest Light," designed by artist Melani Darrell who enjoys traveling and blending the colors of the world into her paintings, is a snapshot of this beautiful state. The sparkling ocean, abundant natural resources and crystal-clear sky come alive in this fanciful rendition of Maine's rock-bound coast. This lighthouse has special meaning since Mitchell scholars—all extraordinary young people—represent the bright future of Maine!

Sponsor:
Clark Associates Insurance

Artist:
James A. Taliana

Clark Associates is a Trusted Choice Insurance Agency, selling and servicing all types of insurance for over 25 well-respected companies. With clients ranging from small and large businesses to individuals and families, Clark Associates takes great pride in delivering the highest quality products to its clients.

Reminiscent of Maine's historic past, "Map Light" is beautifully designed to replicate an antique map of the state's southern coast. Well-known local artist James A. Taliana used latex paints and a urethane coating to create the lighthouse's decorative illustrations—including an old windjammer and ornate compass. All town names featured on the "map" are hand-lettered in calligraphy.

THE MELODRAMATIC LOBSTER

Sponsor:
Brunswick High School

Artists:
Ryan Dougherty, Stephanie Metarelis and Rhea Zerr

Brunswick High School is pleased to support this exciting community art event! Located in coastal Maine, Brunswick High School is dedicated to excellence in academics and the arts. The school also takes pride in encouraging the personal growth of each student.

"The Melodramatic Lobster," which is painted in acrylics, provides a view of coastal Maine with an interesting twist. Artists Ryan Dougherty, Stephanie Metarelis and Rhea Zerr collaborated to create a design using traditional Maine icons that challenge viewers to question their vision. Advanced art students assisted in painting this lighthouse. The Brunswick High Service Learning Class helped fund the project—and Maine Vocational Regional 10 supplied the finishing coat of sealer.

Artists Assisted By:
D.J. Briere, Julie LaChance, Alicia Lussier, Hannah Seluke and Mike Sfirri

Special Thanks To:
An anonymous lighthouse donor who made it possible for Brunswick High School to contribute to the Greater Portland community

Right Page: Detail from "Portland Herd Light"

Sponsor:
USA TELEPHONE

Artist:
Ann Legg

USA TELEPHONE is proud to be a sponsor of Lighthouses on Parade, which personifies the spirit of its mission statement. The Kennebunk-based company believes that improving the lives of customers is about more than providing quality services. It's about corporate responsibility through positive contributions to the community. USA TELEPHONE also fulfills its commitment to community by delivering low-cost local and long distance voice services as well as Internet access.

"Never Fail: Answering the Call for UnWAVEring Service" portrays the undaunted Maine character, even when buffeted by the threatening forces of nature. Artist Ann Legg, President of the Art Guild of the Kennebunks, worked in acrylic glazes, juxtaposing complementary oranges and blues to create tension and drama. Strong, opposing diagonals also enforce this lighthouse's dynamics.

No Light Weights

Sponsor:
EAS Acosta

Artist:
Tatia DiChiara

Established in 1995, EAS continues to build its reputation as the science-based, performance nutrition leader. The company offers a range of products catering to professional athletes, fitness trainers and many other fitness and health enthusiasts.

The design for "No Light Weights" portrays that a lighthouse must be steadfast—there's no room for lightweights! Artist Tatia DiChiara collaborated with her father and engineer, William Squiers, to shape, sculpt and attach bodybuilder's arms to this lighthouse. It was then sanded, sprayed with automotive primer and painted with acrylic enamel. Weights crafted from wood and an oh-so-cool cap are the perfect finishing touches for this "bulked up" lighthouse!

Engineer: William Squiers

OCEAN WONDERS

Sponsor:
Preti Flaherty

Artists:
Third-grade students at the
Mabel I. Wilson School in M.S.A.D. #51,
Cumberland and North Yarmouth,
directed by Evan W. Haynes

Preti Flaherty values its long history of community involvement. As one of Maine's largest law firms, Preti Flaherty helps many of the region's most successful companies thrive and grow. The firm's areas of practice include business, technology and franchise law, employment, intellectual property, litigation, energy, environmental and health care plus legislative and regulatory. With more than 70 attorneys, Preti Flaherty has offices in Portland, Augusta, Bath and Concord.

As part of their study of the Gulf of Maine, over 160 students created the captivating sea creatures that appear to be swimming about the surface of "Ocean Wonders." Assisted by local artist Evan W. Haynes, classroom teachers and art teacher Linda Mock, the students primarily used multi-colored papers and acrylic paints to bring this lighthouse's underwater life...well, to life!

Students Led By:
Classroom teachers and art teacher Linda Mock

Sponsor:
Downeaster Rail Service and Concord Trailways

Artist:
Maureen Farr, Mozelle

Downeaster Rail Service and Concord Trailways are pleased to support the arts community and local charities. Located in the Portland Transportation Center, both Downeaster Rail Service and Concord Trailways provide quality public transportation services.

"People Movers," created by Maureen Farr— a freelance graphic designer and gallery owner—features a colorful, fun-filled and interactive design. A conductor, bus driver and two passengers are painted in acrylics on the lighthouse's middle section. When this section is rotated, the figures' heads, torsos and feet can be mixed and matched! A bus, train, sky with clouds, rising sun and glittery stars add to this lighthouse's whimsical appeal.

Sponsor:
Union Oil Company and Foods on the Go

Artist:
Ian Factor

As one of Greater Portland's largest fuel oil dealers, family-owned Union Oil Company is pleased to participate in this worthy community art event. Serving Maine for over 80 years, the company strives for excellence—and practices its philosophy of guaranteed customer satisfaction—every day. Union Oil Company also encourages its employees to take pride in the community by becoming involved with civic and charitable organizations.

Created by Ian Factor, a local artist whose paintings are popular in the United States and Europe, "The People of Portland" joins together adults and children of all races and religions into one fluid image. The design of this lighthouse reinforces Union Oil Company's function as a quality provider of heating and fuel products—and is a statement of "union" for the people of Portland and the world.

Sponsor:
Peoples Heritage Bank

Artist:
Phyllis Wolf Wilkins

As Maine's largest independent statewide bank, Peoples Heritage Bank places a strong emphasis on community partnerships—making Lighthouses on Parade a natural fit! In addition to bringing pleasure to so many by celebrating a wonderful part of Maine's heritage, this community art event results in significant contributions to Portland-area charities.

Since children are a special focus of the bank and its employees, "Peoples Fireflies" helps bring the bank's charitable giving program to life: People Promise, Shining the Light for Maine Youth. Phyllis Wolf Wilkins—a professional artist who has shown her work throughout New England over the past 14 years—used a mix of latex and acrylic paints, glitter and holiday lights to create this lighthouse's colorful and interactive design. "Peoples Fireflies" captures the childhood spirit of joy and exploration on a summer evening in Maine.

PHOENIX — RESURGENCE OF PORTLAND

Sponsors:
Portland Harbor Hotel and
Portland Downtown District

Artist:
Joshua 2, Dark Horse Designs

The Portland Harbor Hotel is a newfound gem for Old Port area accommodations. Open since July 2002, this stylish boutique property featuring 100 guest rooms is the only luxury hotel in Portland offering Four Diamond services.

Portland's Downtown District is the leader and facilitator in supporting and promoting the economic vitality of downtown Portland. The District produces special events and marketing programs throughout the year to attract people to the area. In addition, it ensures that the downtown Portland environment is clean, safe and friendly.

"Phoenix—Resurgence of Portland" was created by Joshua 2, owner of Dark Horse Designs. Covered with canvas, this fascinating lighthouse depicts a variety of Maine's breathtaking scenes—including Cape Elizabeth and a pier overlooking the ocean. The artist used oil paints, cut metal and wooden structures to give the viewer an impression of "being part of the landscape."

Sponsor:
Oakhurst Dairy

Artist:
Roger C. Williams

Oakhurst Dairy is northern New England's largest dairy company. Operated by the Bennett family since 1921, Oakhurst milk comes from local farms that pledge not to use artificial growth hormones in their products. Since Oakhurst Dairy donates 10% of pre-tax sales dollars each year to help children and the environment, it views Lighthouses on Parade as a great way to have fun while giving back to the community!

A humorous interpretation of the Portland Head Light, "Portland Herd Light" playfully incorporates a herd of cartoon-style cows in a field. Artist Roger C. Williams, known for his commercial as well as fine art, used a colorful mix of acrylic paints to create this lighthouse. It even features a light at the top, representing a galaxy of planets, and a cow jumping over the moon!

Sponsor:
B&M Baked Beans,
a Division of B&G Foods, Inc.

Artist:
Eleda H. Cote,
Mountain Magick Studios

Established in 1867, B&M Baked Beans is a cornerstone of the Portland community. Using only the finest ingredients in manufacturing baked beans and brown bread, B&M's traditional New England-style products are stirred by hand and slow-baked in brick ovens.

Featuring a collage of postcards and bumper stickers—some painted on a background of pine boughs—"Postcards From Maine" depicts area landmarks, destinations and icons. Eleda H. Cote chose a mix of golden acrylics and plates of Maine mica to bring this lighthouse to life...and encourage people to stop and read about all the interesting places to visit in Maine!

THE POWER OF WOMEN, THE DREAMS OF GIRLS

Sponsor:
Maine Women's Fund

Artists:
5th through 12th grade girls, directed by Melissa Pritchard

Maine Women's Fund works diligently to support organizations that assist women and girls statewide—yet many people are still unaware of its existence. By playing a vital role in raising and allocating funds to worthy organizations fostering self-determination, economic empowerment, prevention of violence and improved health, Maine Women's Fund is a beacon of hope for women and girls of all ages and backgrounds.

Melissa Pritchard, a freelance designer and illustrator based in Portland, wanted to help Maine Women's Fund gain awareness. Along with a group of dedicated 5th through 12th grade girls, Melissa began work on "The Power of Women, The Dreams of Girls." This lighthouse is a fitting tribute to the diverse groups and agencies served by Maine Women's Fund—and reflects the dreams of girls everywhere.

Underwritten By:
Sibyl Masquelier of mediahunter.com,
an executive recruiting company for the media industry

Sponsor:
Out Front Productions

Artists:
Dan Edwards and Art Barn artists

In partnership with Hannaford Bros. Co., Out Front Productions is pleased to bring Lighthouses on Parade to the Greater Portland community! Established by Lauren Dixon and Howie Jacobson, Out Front Productions develops and oversees community art projects from coast to coast that "spark" community spirit and creativity. These innovative programs promote tourism, pride—and generate hundreds of thousands of dollars for local charities.

"Reaching for the Stars" was created by Dan Edwards and a group of artists from the Art Barn, an award-winning animation, illustration and Web design studio. A tribute to the 2003 Dodge AHL All-Star Classic hosted by the Portland Pirates, this lighthouse is sure to be a crowd-pleaser. It features 60 stars signed by the All-Stars' players and coaches. Talk about scoring big at the live auction!

Sponsor:
WCSH-6 TV

Artist:
John LeBlanc

WCSH-6, Portland's NBC-TV affiliate, is celebrating 50 years of local broadcasting during 2003. More Mainers watch the station's top-rated newscasts than any other source. WCSH-6 takes pride in the community and welcomes the opportunity to support its charities. The station also wanted to capitalize on its prominent downtown location—the perfect lighthouse display site!

Noted Maine artist John LeBlanc has created a "Reunion" of the area's most picturesque lighthouses. Since choosing one of these historic landmarks was impossible, a collection of them is gathered together and wonderfully illustrated in this colorful "garden" of lighthouses.

Sponsor:
Purdy Powers & Company

Artist:
Hannah Nelsbach

Purdy Powers & Company offers accounting, tax and business advisory services designed to increase clients' productivity and profitability over the long term. From preparing financial statements and tax returns to complex planning, management studies and business valuations, Purdy Powers & Company provides the level of service required to start—and keep—your business moving in the right direction!

Designed by Hannah Nelsbach, a local artist whose goal is to make the world more colorful, "The Right Direction" displays the mariner's heritage of charting rough seas. With a steady, confident hand on the helm, the Purdy Powers & Company crew is always here to guide your ship in the right direction! A skipper's alphabet, seabirds and underwater life complete this dynamic lighthouse.

SAFE HARBOR LIGHT

Sponsors:
Newman's Own, Inc. and Camp Sunshine

Artist:
Marsha Donahue, Greenhut Galleries

Since its inception in 1982, Newman's Own, Inc. has achieved a stellar reputation with its range of distinctive, high-quality foods and philanthropic mission. Paul Newman credits much of the success of his company to the fact that he donates all after-tax profits from product sales to educational and charitable organizations. As Newman himself has often quipped, "From salad dressing all blessings flow."

"Safe Harbor Light" is a tribute to Camp Sunshine—a retreat located in Sebago, Maine—where children with life-threatening illnesses and their families can find light in the darkness. Created by artist Marsha Donahue, with assistance from her brother Glenn Hinckley, this colorful lighthouse with three-dimensional highlights symbolically depicts children clinging to a life preserver in deep and stormy waters.

Technical Assistance:
Glenn Hinckley

Right Page: Detail from "Ocean Wonders"

Sponsor:
Samantha Odwalla Inc.

Artist:
Abby Carter

Samantha Odwalla Inc. welcomes the opportunity to support the Portland community and its artists! As a leading manufacturer of super-premium refrigerated juices, the company distributes its products coast to coast. Customers can depend on Samantha Odwalla for juices that are always fresh, never from concentrate and preservative-free!

The whimsical "Samantha Goes to 'C'" features Samantha and her dog Willy-Boy enjoying a sail in their bright yellow boat. The two seagoers are surrounded by many colorful friends. Designed by Abby Carter, a freelance illustrator and creator of the Samantha character, this delightful lighthouse will bring a smile to everyone's face!

Sponsor:
Dead River Company

Artist:
Diane Bragdon

Dead River Company, one of the largest retailers of home heating oil and propane in northern New England, strongly believes in community involvement and supporting charitable organizations. "Security" is a fitting name for this lighthouse sponsored by Dead River—since the company has delivered a reliable and plentiful supply of petroleum products to its customers for over 60 years.

Working on a ten-foot, three-dimensional canvas enabled Diane Bragdon to "create outside the box." An accomplished watercolor artist, she drew upon her Maine surroundings to develop the design for "Security." A vibrant mix of acrylic paints were then used to playfully incorporate Dead River trucks that are "always in the neighborhood," providing security and comfort.

Septaquintaquinquecentennial Light (175th Anniversary)

Sponsor:
Saco & Biddeford Savings Institution

Artist:
Amy Cote,
Hand Painting for All Occasions

Saco & Biddeford Savings Institution is pleased to take part in this high-visibility community event! For 175 years, Saco & Biddeford has lived up to its slogan, "You know us. We know you," by being loyal to its customers, employees and the community. As Maine's oldest mutual savings bank, Saco & Biddeford prides itself on delivering quality financial products and superior customer service.

"Septaquintaquinquecentennial Light" depicts the ocean seascapes of Maine, focusing on the fishing industry and life along the coast. Artist Amy Cote used paint, sand, pennies, wood and a host of other materials to create this lighthouse. A self-portrait of Amy painting eye-catching scenes—and a rotating beacon light—complete the design.

Sponsor:
Spencer Press Inc.

Artists:
Jay Piscopo and David Roberts

Spencer Press is pleased to participate in Lighthouses on Parade and support local charities. A privately owned commercial printer located in Wells, Maine since 1982, Spencer Press is known for its annual calendar highlighting the beauty and timelessness of lighthouses worldwide. The 63-year-old company also prints 600 million retail and direct-mail catalogs per year.

Designed by Jay Piscopo and David Roberts, "Serene Passage" resembles a page from the Spencer Press calendar where the lighthouse is the focal point, surrounded by a breathtaking landscape. A colorful mix of sign paints brings this lighthouse's seascape—complete with sailboats and rocky coast of Maine—to life.

SHIPYARD LIGHT

Sponsor:
The Shipyard Brewing Company

**Official Beer of
Lighthouses on Parade**

Artists:
Jay Piscopo and David Roberts

Hannaford's Lighthouses on Parade is a perfect fit for The Shipyard Brewing Company's philosophy of corporate giving. The Shipyard Brewing Company is the leading craft brewery in the northeast—and has been handcrafting fine ales with a wide range of profiles since 1994.

Jay Piscopo used his signature painted wood sculpture and whimsical folk art style to perfectly capture The Shipyard Brewing Company's family of products depicted on "Shipyard Light." He was assisted by David Roberts, a Web designer and musician with carpentry and sign painting experience. The design of this lighthouse, which is based on old-fashioned advertising displays, provides a glimpse of The Shipyard Brewing Company's past as well as its vision for the future.

Right Page: Detail from "Shipyard Light"

STRENGTH ON YOUR SIDE

Sponsor:
General Dynamics Armament and Technical Products

Artist:
Piper Bolduc

With a proud tradition of designing, manufacturing and assembling ordnance-related products, General Dynamics Armament and Technical Products is pleased to contribute to the important charities that will benefit from Lighthouses on Parade. Sponsoring "Strength on Your Side" will help bolster pride in employees and visitors who will be enjoying the events and publicity throughout the summer.

Besides being a project that will benefit so many, full-time art teacher and local artist Piper Bolduc couldn't resist painting on a sculpture that's cherished as a "Mainer"—the lighthouse. "Strength on Your Side" features a hand-painted design that combines patriotic elements with a central image of a fishing harbor along the Maine coast. Medallions showcase persons, places, products and resources synonymous with the "total Maine experience."

Sponsor:
Canandaigua Wine Company

Artist:
Hannah Nelsbach

Canandaigua Wine Company, a leading provider of wines in Maine, is delighted to participate in this worthy community art project. By sponsoring "Sunset Fiesta," the company is able to give back to the community while shining a new light on its products. Each year, Canandaigua Wine ships over 600,000 gallons of wine to retail locations and restaurants throughout Maine.

Using latex and acrylic paints, Hannah Nelsbach captured a sunset scene on a Maine beach. A picnic complete with colorful tablecloth, lobster, mussels, bread and, of course, wine, adds to the festive design of "Sunset Fiesta."

UNDERCOVER LIGHTHOUSE

Sponsor:
Lighthouse Depot

Artists:
Lighthouse Depot Staff, directed by Joan Prentice

As the world's largest lighthouse gift store, Lighthouse Depot believes this worthy community art project featuring a parade of lighthouses is a natural fit! Based in Wells, Maine, Lighthouse Depot also publishes a mail-order catalog that reaches six million people worldwide. Its Web site, www.lighthousedepot.com, offers a history on lighthouses as well as books, collectibles, clothing and a host of other lighthouse-related products for sale.

Appropriately named "Undercover Lighthouse," this "secret agent" dons clothing made from the store's catalog covers, dating back to its first issue in 1994. Lighthouse Depot's talented employees, led by assistant store manager Joan Prentice, designed the lighthouse. Just imagine the fun this secret agent will have searching for lost lighthouse history and new products!

Sponsor:
Greater Portland
Chambers of Commerce

Artists:
Ed Jarrett and Leolyn Wood

All of us at the Greater Portland Chambers of Commerce are pleased to "Welcome" Hannaford's Lighthouses on Parade to our region! Representing over 1,300 member companies, the Greater Portland Chambers of Commerce is the largest business membership organization in Maine that strives to enhance regional economic performance through business and civic leadership.

"Welcome," designed by artists Ed Jarrett and Leolyn Wood, is a true reflection of all the advantages of living and working in Greater Portland. It is a city of historic charm mixed with new technology. One with a proud past and a bright future. And what better way to demonstrate this than by showing Portland, a land of vast opportunity, at the end of this lighthouse's colorful rainbow!

WILBUR'S CHOCOLATE LIGHTS THE WAY

Sponsor:
Wilbur's of Maine
Chocolate Confections

Artists:
Laura Baecher, Amber Lambke
and Catherine Conway

Since its founding in 1983, Wilbur's of Maine Chocolate Confections has focused on providing the finest quality chocolate at the best possible price. From blueberry creams made with fresh Maine berries to delicious caramels made with dairy cream to chocolate-covered blueberries and cranberries, Wilbur's is known for its old-fashioned goodness. Wilbur's is also delighted to ship its chocolates anywhere in the U.S. when orders are placed online at www.wilburs.com.

The red-and-white striped "Wilbur's Chocolate Lights the Way," designed by Laura Baecher, Amber Lambke and Catherine Conway, is modeled after Wilbur's logo. A mix of blueberries, lobsters and shells—symbols of Maine as well as confections offered by Wilbur's—add to this lighthouse's appeal.

Sponsor:
The American Lighthouse Foundation (ALF)
Technical and Historical Advisor for Lighthouses on Parade

Artist:
John Byrne

The American Lighthouse Foundation (ALF), a non-profit lighthouse preservation group, wanted to participate in this community art event. However, the organization's by-laws require that funds be used for preservation purposes only. Fortunately, LITEHOUSE Foods and The Shipyard Brewing Company stepped forward. A portion of the proceeds from sales of LITEHOUSE Foods dressings, dips and sauces and Shipyard Light Ale—as well as the sale of this book—go to ALF to help save our nation's historic lighthouses.

"Ye Beacons" purpose is to draw attention to ALF—and encourage people to donate or join the all-volunteer organization. Designed by John Byrne, known for his signature photo artistry, this lighthouse features 100 nautical images that shine new light on the majesty of America's lighthouses. The artist hired a mathematician to determine angles for placing flat prints on the lighthouse's conical surface.

Underwritten By:
LITEHOUSE Foods and
The Shipyard Brewing Company

YOUR SHIP HAS COME IN

Sponsor:
The Shipyard Brewing Company

Official Beer of
Lighthouses on Parade

Artist:
John Byrne

As a long-time supporter of the arts and Portland area non-profit organizations, Shipyard Brewing Company sees Lighthouses on Parade as a logical extension of its strong beliefs to give back to the community. The Shipyard Brewing Company has been making fine ales since 1994—and uses only top-quality ingredients to create the consistency and fresh taste that sets its beer apart!

Designed by John Byrne, a musician, sculptor and photomontage artist, "Your Ship Has Come In" is an elaborate photographic history of everything that contributes to The Shipyard Brewing Company's uniqueness. This intriguing lighthouse is covered with nearly 100 nautical and beer-related images.

Right Page: Detail from "The Lights of Maine

OWLS HEAD LIGHT
BUILT 1825

URRELL POINT LIGHT
BUILT 1898

DOUBLING
POINT LIGHT BUILT 1898

THE C

LIGHT
BUILT
855

CAPE NEDDICK (NUBBLE LIGHT)
BUILT 1879

Detail from "King Crustacean"

INDEX BY SPONSOR

Detail from "The Power of Women, The Dreams of Girls"

INDEX BY ARTIST

Detail from "Never Fail: Answering the Call for UnWAVEring Service"

INDEX BY LIGHTHOUSE

OFFICIAL SPONSORS AND ACKNOWLEDGEMENTS

LIGHTHOUSES ON PARADE HAS BEEN MADE POSSIBLE THANKS TO THE GENEROUS SUPPORT OF OUR OFFICIAL SPONSORS:

HANNAFORD BROS. CO., our Presenting Sponsor

BULLY HILL WINERY, Official Wine

CHOICE ONE COMMUNICATIONS, Official Web Developer

HAVEN'S CANDIES, Official Confectioner

PORTLAND PRESS HERALD/MAINE SUNDAY TELEGRAM, Official Media Partner

THE SHIPYARD BREWING COMPANY, Official Beer

A special thank you to the following people and companies for their donation of time, materials, space, manpower and overall hard work. Lighthouses on Parade is a huge success because of all of you! We would also like to extend our appreciation to the many community members not mentioned below who have embraced this project.

CITY OF PORTLAND:

Alan Holt for a tremendous job in coordinating all city agencies involved with this project.
Mayor James F. Cloutier
Karen Geraghty

SOUTH PORTLAND:

Jeff Jordan, City Manager

South Portland Fire Department—great neighbors to have!

Michael Drinan from the Waterfront Market Association, who provided information for the South Portland area.

Steve Smith from Hannaford Bros. Co. for his vision.

Fred Forsley and Tami Kennedy from The Shipyard Brewing Company for their unwavering support and donation of warehouse space for unfinished lighthouses.

Mariner's Church Banquet Center for providing an artist design showcase location.

Michael J. Mahoney of M&M Entertainment for providing DJ services at Lighthouses on Parade events.

PORTLAND DOWNTOWN DISTRICT:

Rena Masten
Keely Cameron

Advisory Committee:

Julia Bell	Alan Holt
Mark Charest	Michelle Johns
James F. Cloutier	Barbara Keefe
Jackie Cohen	Lynn Ann MacGregor
George and Joan Connick	Richard Paulson, Jr.
Jon Connick	Kathy Powers
Christine Force	Toni Richardson
Fred Frawley	Michael Shaughnessy
Karen Geraghty	Bonnie Titcomb
Evan Haynes	Lisa Veleff

OUR PHOTOGRAPHERS:

Dennis and Diana Griggs of Tannery Hill Studios. Thank you for making photography fun!

Pauline M. Dimino, our behind-the-scenes photographer.

ADDITIONAL ASSISTANCE PROVIDED BY:

Tatia DiChiara, Joshua 2 and Dave Karl Roberts, talented Lighthouses on Parade artists who also helped move lighthouses during the photo shoot.

William Squiers for making lighthouse "shoes" and moving platform.

Garrett Richardson for manning the lighthouse pick-up location.

John Holverson and Bob Golden from Museum of Glass and Ceramics for providing our lighthouses with a home!

Fred Frawley from Preti Flaherty for offering the very best in legal services as well as the use of the firm's beautiful conference rooms.

The Portland Expo, The Boulos Company and Upscale Consignment Furniture, Inc. for donating artist space.

Headlight Audio Visual, Inc. for providing expert A/V services at Lighthouses on Parade events—and for always pitching in to help move a lighthouse!

Laurie Hyndman and Kelly Ericson from Port City Life for their enthusiastic support of this project.

Tim Harrison, President of The American Lighthouse Foundation—an invaluable source on everything relating to lighthouses!

The Eastland Park Hotel and the Portland Harbor Hotel for providing us a home while in Portland.

The Maine Center on Deafness for arranging to have sign language interpreters at all Lighthouses on Parade events.

Mr. and Mrs. Conneen for giving the Out Front Productions team a beautiful place to stay!

Godfrey Wood and Pete Ventre from the Greater Portland Chambers of Commerce —a big thank you for welcoming us to your city!

Prewitt-Fiberglass for providing the 10-foot tall lighthouses.

Vicky Ferentz for providing us with background information about Portland.

Grace Jacobson for working with us during the summer of 2002 to get this project rolling!

Michael Townsend from Golden Artist Colors for providing excellent technical support as well as speaking at the artist workshop.

Michael Shaughnessy from the University of Southern Maine, Gorham Campus for allowing us to use their sculptor studio for the artist workshop.

Artist and Craftsman Supply for offering a discount on supplies to all Lighthouses on Parade artists.

Brenda Libby from Saco Spirit, Inc. for her enthusiastic support of this project!

The Maine Mall for providing our sponsors with lighthouse locations.

Professor Charles S. Colgan and his students at University of Southern Maine's Edmund S. Muskie School of Public Service for their assistance in gathering of economic impact research.

Charlene Belanger for including the Lighthouses on Parade works of art in the Maine State Parade.

Portland Museum of Art and Maine Arts Commission for helping to put us in touch with the talented artists of Maine who brought the lighthouses to life!

Lobstering

Ship Building

Old Orchard Pier

Detail from "Strength on Your Side"

121

Memorable Maine Moments

MY MOST TREASURED MEMORIES OF MAINE ARE…

_____

_____

_____

_____

_____

Paste favorite 4" x 6" Maine photo here

MY FAVORITE HISTORIC LIGHTHOUSE WAS…

_____

WHEN I DREAM OF MAINE, IT'S ABOUT…

_____

_____

_____

_____

STAYED AT...

_____

_____

_____

_____

_____

_____

_____

_____

Paste favorite 4" x 6" Maine photo here

ATE MY FIRST MAINE LOBSTER AT..._____

TOOK LONG WALKS ALONG THE BEACH AT..._____

Paste favorite 4" x 6" Maine photo here

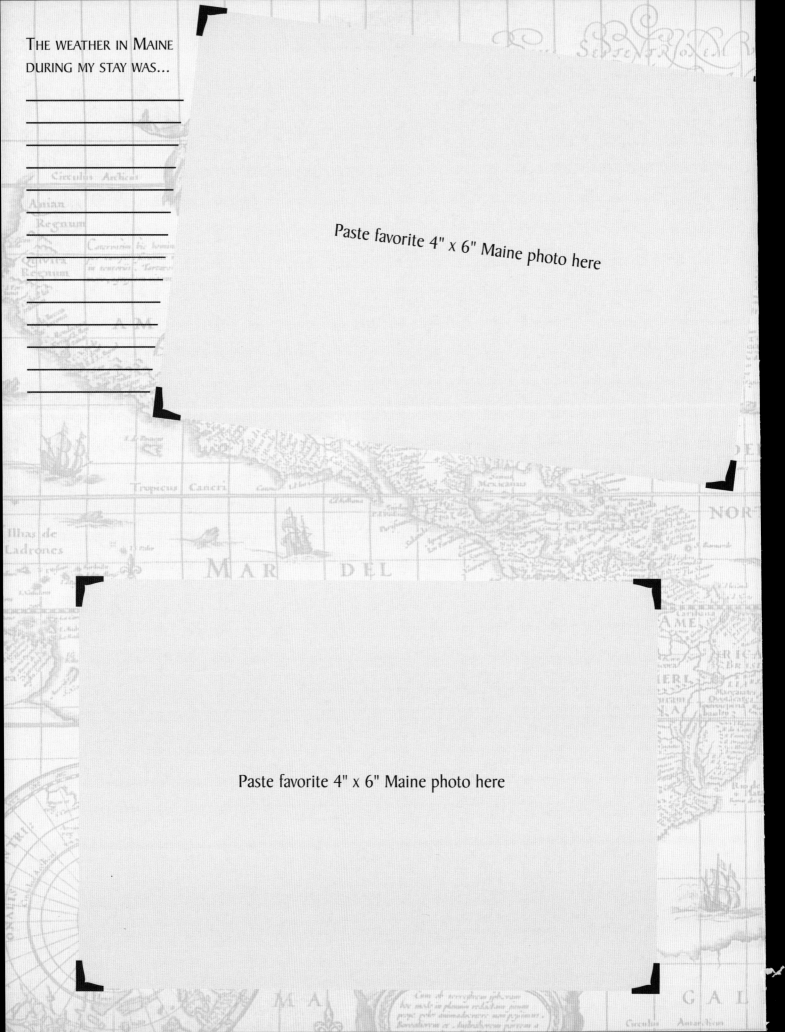

THE WEATHER IN MAINE
DURING MY STAY WAS...

_____
_____
_____
_____

_____

_____

_____

_____

Paste favorite 4" x 6" Maine photo here

Paste favorite 4" x 6" Maine photo here

SOME INTERESTING THINGS I LEARNED ABOUT MAINE ARE...

_____

_____

_____

_____

Paste favorite 4" x 6" Maine photo here

MY FAVORITE RESTAURANT WAS...

_____

_____

_____

MY FAVORITE LIGHTHOUSES ON PARADE WORKS OF ART WERE...

_____

_____

_____

_____